RECESS TIME

The Best Cartoons from the *Kappan*

Edited by Kristin Herzog

Published by Phi Delta Kappa
P.O. Box 789, Bloomington, IN 47402

©1983 by Phi Delta Kappa

All rights reserved.

Library of Congress Catalog Card Number 83-062201

ISBN 0-87367-788-9

Cover illustration by Jim Hull

Book design by Kristin Herzog

Foreword

My job as editor of the *Kappan* requires that I travel a great deal — many times to speak to chapters of Phi Delta Kappa or to other groups of readers. Sooner or later at one of these gatherings, someone will say, "You know what I like best about the *Kappan*? The cartoons!" I must admit that the editor part of me — that part that wants the *Kappan* to be a valued source of information — is always a bit dismayed by this inevitable comment. But that part of me that reads the cartoons in the *New Yorker* before anything else understands completely — and secretly nods agreement.

We always enjoy receiving a new batch of cartoons. We receive many more than we're able to use, of course. No one person here decides which cartoons we'll publish; we pass them around and each editor (as well as our marvelous design director, Kris Herzog) gets a vote. In compiling this collection of the best cartoons from the *Kappan*, all four of us — myself, Kris, Pauline Gough, and Bruce Smith — voted on every cartoon that we've published in the past 13 years. We hope that we've included your favorites. I know that the task brightened our summer.

Sometimes some of our readers will object to a particular cartoon, claiming that it derides one segment or another of the education profession. I'll admit that our cartoonists' humor can be rather barbed at times, but it seems important to me that all of us be able to laugh at ourselves amid the awful seriousness of our work. It's healthy. Education may not be funny, but people certainly are.

Robert W. Cole, Jr.
Editor
Phi Delta Kappan

A Student's Life

"*Who says school doesn't prepare us for the real world? We're already learning double digits.*"

"Hey, dad! Can I borrow Bossy for geography class?"

"You'll be sorry you made me study so hard when I'm overeducated and unemployed!"

"*What a coincidence!* I'm *majoring in something ending in 'ology' too.*"

"Recess is my most important subject. I'm going to be a congressman."

2/83

3/80

"She told me to clean out my desk, so I assumed I was fired."

"What did I learn today? My mother will want to know."

10/82

6/82

"Here's my test, Mr. Sauer. I've left a few intentional mistakes. I wonder if you'll be able to find them."

"Has anybody seen the tarantula I brought for 'show and tell'?"

1/80

"Herby Murdock won't be bringing his botany project in on time. He was booked for possession of it."

4/71

" 'Adventures in Literature' is on at 9:30; at 10:00 we have 'French for Everyone,' followed by a rerun of 'Concepts of Chemistry'. . ."

"How do you get to be a knight? You have to go to knight school."

5/82

"What do I get for just neatness?"

5/78

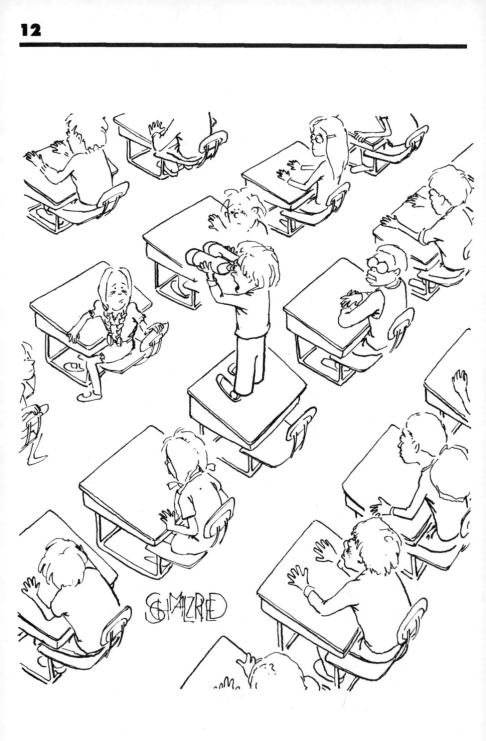

"I . . . I think I can make out the teacher!"

"Can you imagine? At some schools they make you wear a uniform."

3/82

"Hey, everybody! Look what followed me to school!"

2/78

"*Use my mind? At home?*"

"I'm in love with Miss Scott, but she's only interested in me for my mind."

11/82

"Certainly we can answer the question, 'How much is six times nine?' May I ask who's calling?"

12/81

"I'll probably never get rubbed out for knowing too much."

4/83

12/78

SHOW AND TELL

"Timmy, your father's out in the hall. He wants to talk to you about borrowing without asking."

5/80

NOT A THROUGH STREET

"When do you suppose they'll be through with it?"

11/82

"I know my seven-digit phone number, my nine-digit zip code, my four-digit address, and my three-digit area code. There's just one thing I don't know. What's a digit?"

"A boy with a classical education, I suppose."

6/80

"I'm in kindergarten — kind of testing the educational waters."

5/81

"*Now that we know how to read, they're banning all the good stuff.*"

10/82

"*Let's pretend he didn't charge it, Philip. . . .*"

"*Course, it's just a ballpark figure.*"

"But if I go every day, won't I wear out my welcome?"

"It's not easy getting all your homework done between dinnertime and prime time."

3/80

" 'My Summer,' by Elizabeth Pennypacker. I spent the early part of my summer in Rochester, N.Y., with my daddy while he switched jobs, the middle part of my summer in Reno with my mom while she switched husbands, and the last part of my summer in Denmark with my big brother while he switched sexes."

9/75

"This would be a lot easier if they didn't require such pinpoint accuracy."

"Want me to move along?"

9/82

"It's terrible being a TV viewer trapped in the body of a student."

1/83

"Hello, I'm Billy Bernard — part of the mess you inherited from the previous administration."

"*Everything's gone up.*"

4/82

"*But I haven't got time to use context clues to figure out which is which. . . .*"

12/76

"*Do you want me to be the only nonviewer in a nation of nonreaders?*"

"Hey, mom! This guy says he's on the show to plug his book. What's a book?"

3/83

"I knew the answers. I just couldn't retrieve them from my memory bank."

9/82

"*The third-grade crisis . . . day 53. . . .*"

"Mrs. Horton, could you stop by school today?"

6/81

"Deer Mom, Wud you belive I lost my job at the offise today? I gess sumwun thair doesnt like me."

5/73

"I consider myself well prepared for college. My family has money."

5/83

GRADE 4

"Susan B. Anthony was an American woman minted in nineteen seventy-nine. . . ."

12/81

Dealing With Parents

"*You are a Webster and Websters are conservative, Episcopalian, and Republican, and go to Exeter, Princeton, and into the family business.*"

"Yoo hoo, Harold! Time to come in and wash up and get ready for college!"

"*This is a metric cookbook. Do you have a grade schooler who can read it to you?*"

1/81

"*You've got to stop being so listless in class. I* never *heard of someone getting an incomplete in conduct!*"

11/74

"Remember the good old days of campus unrest and takeovers, sit-ins, confrontations, obscenity, bombings, disrespect for the established institutions, rudeness, long hair, harassment, pot, sexual liberation, and utter disregard for the rights of others?"

6/76

"We might as well face it. We're a middle-of-the-road, middle-income, median-grade-level family."

3/82

"It would be more appropriate if you had your hand in my pocket."

"Your worries are over, Pop. The school has a major for heirs apparent."

"Okay kids, your tutor's here."

3/77

"Then my parents broke down and told me the truth. Those weren't field trips after all. I was being bused."

9/73

"It's been three months now, son! How about it — ready for bigger things?"

6/82

"The subject was inexplicable, so I didn't try to explick it."

"Well, Gramps, I guess when I grow up I want the Great American Dream: to become a hot property that's exploited shamelessly in commercials, fast foods, T-shirts, TV, games, toys, novelties, and breakfast cereals to the tune of 1.2 million dollars a year."

"Now what?"

"Don't you think your Holt, Rinehart & Winstons would go well with your Calvins and your Nikes?"

"No, I'm not working my way through college. I'm helping my father pay back his student loan."

"Well, you see, Mrs. Smith, the reason your son is doing poorly in school is that he's dumb."

11/72

"Complimentary verbalization is nice, Mom, but I'd prefer the compensatory approach."

4/83

"I understand you've achieved name recognition in the principal's office."

"Because being a student is your societal role. That's why you have to go to school."

"It's not exactly a note from the teacher. It's more like a joint communiqué from the faculty."

3/81

"Continue to support sex education in the schools if you want to, but Billy just told me that he resulted when your sperm met my omelet."

4/83

Teachers

"I'm not an underachiever. You're an overexpecter."

"Of course it's misspelled. I'm preserving my indigenous cultural dialect."

11/79

". . . and the reason we have summer vacation is so you can go home to help with the crops."

6/80

"*Mr. Sproul is always coming up with something new in the way of an interest center.*"

4/75

"*I'd like to overwhelm them with instructional excellence, but I'm not above winning through intimidation.*"

2/81

"*Ah, I see Miss Tupman has started her elementary sex education class. . . .*"

4/76

"*I'm not sure I like science in the classroom. They're trying to figure out my age through carbon dating.*"

6/76

Schmalzried

"I'm not sure just what we're observing, but the smaller ones are obviously in control."

"*I welcome you to our meeting on the handicapped. I can see that some of us are not too familiar with the mainstreaming concept.*"

12/81

"*Please feel free to call on me if any of you think you need individual attention.*"

5/83

"*I can't tell you what a relief it is to relax after a year of teaching!*"

3/79

"*I'm taking an innovative approach to teaching this semester. I'm using books!*"

2/78

"I'm a teacher . . . I teach first grade . . . I like children . . . children like me . . . do you like children? I have a dog . . . My dog is brown . . . My dog's name is Rover . . ."

"It's moments like this — when they're all so very, very quiet — that I get a strange, uneasy feeling."

"This is Wally. He's representing us in our homework negotiations."

1/76

"And now we'll need someone to erase the blackboard. Who has only a master's degree?"

5/75

"If you ask me, Buster, you're just a little too literate for your own good."

5/79

"This is merit pay?"

"Horsey. Horsey big. Horsey go giddyap."

"Prof. Howland is a gentleman and a scholar — but not at the same time."

"Shh — Dr. Gottlieb is writing the biggest number he can think of."

9/76

AND NOW, CLASS, A FEW MOMENTS OF PRAYER IN MEMORY OF THE FIRST AMENDMENT...

"*Your feelings of insecurity seem to have started when Mary Lou Gurnblatt said, 'Maybe I don't have a learning disability — maybe you have a teaching disability.'* "

5/75

"*First I slaved to make twenty million dollars. Then I built a small university. It was the easiest way to find a teaching job.*"

12/78

"Boys and girls, today is my last day of teaching after 36 years at Walnut Hills High. Should we chance to meet along life's highway, I shan't correct your English. However, I may very well give you a good swift kick for no apparent reason."

"What kind of field trip is this, anyway?"

"Actually, Mr. Green, after deductions for federal tax, state tax, local tax, F.I.C.A., union dues, insurance premiums, and health insurance — you owe us $6.43."

10/75

"I think I'll take the day off!"

11/80

"Are we that desperate for substitute teachers?"

3/83

"I swear I heard someone say 'meaningfully-wise.'"

5/82

"*And then, of course, there's the possibility of being just the slightest bit* too *organized.*"

"Tommy's bad behavior wouldn't be so intolerable if it weren't for his perfect attendance."

6/77

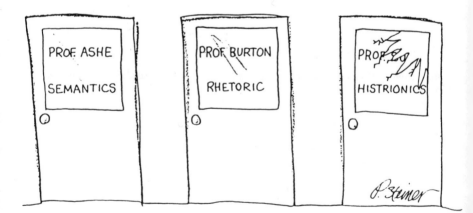

"Jim claims it triples their attention span."

"It's difficult to reprimand some children for inattention in class."

4/80

"Every year Ms. Hawkins applies for an educational block grant."

1/83

"You can't promote me out of the sixth grade. I have tenure!"

4/76

TEACHERS'
LOUNGE

"The kids don't listen, so I have to repeat myself. I'm always repeating myself. You know, always saying the same thing more than once. I say it once, and they make me say it again. . . ."

3/81

"Of course I believe that a teacher should offer a positive role model; however . . ."

4/79

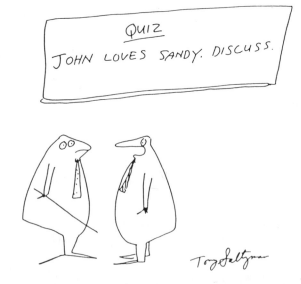

"We feel, Henderson, that your sociology class is concentrating a little too heavily on local issues."

11/70

"Well, I won't believe in an antiparticle until I see one."

"That's Professor Allenbeck. He's occupied the Sterling Chair of Anthropology for 30 years and he rarely leaves it these days."

1/79

"No, I don't get overtime for keeping you after school."

2/83

"*If you will remember, Bobby, I urged you to study harder!*"

"Write me a convincing essay explaining why I should remain your teacher."

"Mirror, mirror, on the wall, who's the most sensitive, open, student-centered, and innovative teacher of all?"

The Administration

"We understand you ignored a federal guideline!"

"There's been some criticism that this college overemphasizes sports. How do you feel about that, Dean Ryan?"

4/77

"Monies allocated for special educational programs came to zero. However, we expect that figure to be matched by federal funds."

9/70

"Our architect has come up with an interesting concept in building design that might create an atmosphere in which students could achieve excellence."

1/75

"Do you want the personnel file on Mr. Perkins that's in the file cabinet or the one in the shoe box in your closet?"

10/75

"*No, Miss Shumway, as a very busy superintendent of schools, I don't have ulcers. I'm a carrier.*"

"Get out of here quick, Mr. Pendleton! The reception room is full of irate teachers folding, spindling, and mutilating!"

2/73

DEPARTMENT OF EDUCATION

DIVISION OF PWESCHOOL PWOGRAMS

5/75

"It's the damned SDS shaking the foundations of American education."

"*Our problem is whether to use the extra funds to hire three security guards or five teachers.*"

3/73

10/82

"The safety patrol has seized power!"

"Why am I worried about maintaining academic standards? For one thing, this is a class on Chaucer."

"Enrollment down?"

". . . and we are working diligently to make this a university our football team can be proud of!"

"There's the guidance counselor. He's lost again."

3/81

BOARD OF EDUCATION

"I've got it! We'll bus the teachers."

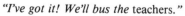

1/83

"Unfortunately, due to cuts in student aid, there is no graduating class."

"Now, do we all have our thinking caps on?"

9/81

"Our next speaker's subject is 'Pitfalls to Avoid in Public School Financial Management.'"

"Have you had any experience working with children?"

10/75

"We'll need more justification for your application for sabbatical leave than just 'A year away from them! A year away from them!'"

"We don't have a leader here -- just our principal, Mr. Langburn."

"The bad news is we're losing enrollment. The good news is we're number three in the NCAA standings on TV!"

12/82

"Our break must be over!"

12/80

"I'm making you chairman of our Ethical Standards Committee."

6/77

"I see our main speaker needs no introduction."

"*Way to go, Russelman!*"

"It's Mr. Jarvis, the truant officer. He found three kids playing hookey. They're holding him for ransom."

1/78

COUNSELOR

"Marry money."

6/73

THE PERAMBULATING
ADVISORY
(Consultantianus Educatorum)

Habitat: Found throughout the educational world. Rarely seen for more than a few hours in one place.

Food: Consumes large quantities of money.

Identifying Characteristics: Fastest of educational mammals. While the myth that it can be in several places at once is not true, it moves rapidly from place to place foraging for food. Faster species members have been clocked at up to eight feeding grounds per day.

THE SNAGGLE-TOOTHED
BUDGETARY
(School Boardium Budgetarius Horribilis)

Habitat: Only visits educational world occasionally. Usually found looking over shoulder of other species.

Food: Source of food lies outside educational ecosystem.

Identifying Characteristics: Tool using. Usually carries shears or blue pencil. Recognizable by its repeated low guttural cry of "coststoomuchcoststoomuchcoststoomuchcoststoomuch!" Deadly enemy of Umbrella-Armed Overhanger, but often shares nest with Strong-Jawed Idea Crusher.

THE BROAD-MOUTHED
DATA CATCHER
(Researchius Educatorum)

Habitat: Difficult to determine because no live member of this species has ever been seen. Evidence of its existence comes from large numbers of forms and tests left for other species. Believed to live on margins of the educational world.

Food: Believed to subsist largely on a diet of numbers.

Identifying Characteristics: Difficult to determine because of lack of sightings. One unverified sighting behind a stack of questionnaires suggests it may have computer terminals in its head.

THE FLITTERING RELEVANT
(Teachorum Trendyius)

Habitat: Builds nests near most popular other species in educational world.

Food: Lives mainly on clichés.

Identifying Characteristics: Remarkable directional sense, thought to come from large ears which can move in 360-degree circle, allows it to move quickly to site of any new activity in educational world. Has no call of its own, but is excellent mimic of other species. Observers report that most frequent call recently has been: 'openstructurednonsexistmulticultural."

THE STRONG-JAWED
IDEA CRUSHER
(Educationus Negativum)

Habitat: Ubiquitous in educational world.

Food: Continually chews ideas, but has never been seen to swallow one. Real source of nourishment is unknown.

Identifying Characteristics: Easily recognizable by its shrill cry of "NoNoNoNoNoNoNoNo." If found in position of authority, it can usually be recognized by the lack of other species in close proximity.

THE BURBLING JARGONEER
(Paedigogicus Incomprehensibilum)

Habitat: Found mainly in schools of education
and offices of educational journals, but evidence
of its influence on other species is seen
throughout the educational world.

Food: Eats mainly Latinate roots.

Identifying Characteristics: Consists exclusively
of large mouth and one paw with single digit
suitable only for pecking at typewriter. Extremely
dangerous to approach. Unwary observers who
have attempted to make sense of its call have
become permanently deranged.

THE YELLOW-NOTED LECTORUM
(Professorus Stupefactium)

Habitat: Found throughout the educational world.

Food: Remarkable recycling process allows this species continually to ingest its own product.

Identifying Characteristics: While it can be most easily identified by the crumpled pieces of paper it clutches between its forepaws, this species can also often be recognized by its continuous emission of jokes first popularized during the Neolithic Era. Mouth is sometimes thought to resemble cassette recorder with tape loop.

THE FURRY-TAILED IDEA HOPPER
(Teachorum Innovatus)

Habitat: Likes unrestricted, unstructured spaces.

Food: Gulps large quantities of gimmicks.

Identifying Characteristics: Always in motion, though it seldom appears to be going anywhere. Inexperienced observers may have difficulty following its rapid jumping from idea to idea. Care should be taken to avoid experimental curricula, activity cards, and other debris which are frequently found in its wake.

Life After School

"You'd think they could do better than, 'These are the bones of a really old lizardy kind of thing.'"

"He's waiting for something to insult his intelligence."

"*The* Phi Delta Kappan *sent me an honorarium, but it's of no consequencium.*"

4/80

5/80

"*Must have been a men's room.*"

6/80

"*Okay, Buster, why can't it be an honest* woman *you're looking for?*"

4/76

"Morton has our opinions readied should Gallup or Harris call."

11/79

10/81

"It's my mantra."

4/78

ENTERING
PRIVATE
SECTOR

10/82

12/79

"This one stops at Fordham, Columbia, N.Y.U. . . . ."

9/81

"Aid to education sounds fine, but you and I know what will happen if the voters get too damned bright."

"I'm trying to locate the annals of time."

10/79

3/80

"Remember when hardware meant a hammer and nails?"

1/83

3/76

"We programmed it to simulate living conditions in the year 2000, and it's become hysterical."

6/80

"I admit TV is educational — it's driving me back to reading books."

3/82

12/77

"Keep an eye out for a smart kid!"

11/75

"It's only a stone's throw from the nearest school."

4/79

"How many times must I tell you — it's 'cat' before 'temple' except after 'slave'."

6/76

10/78

12/77

1/80

6/81

"It's a bookcase. Where's our book?"

11/77

"My intelligence isn't insulted by TV anymore."

© 83 PETT PHI DELTA KAPPAN

"Elwin defaulted on his student loan, so they repossessed his diploma."

The Cartoonists

GLENN BERNHARDT

Glenn Bernhardt is what younger cartoonists refer to as a "veteran." He is currently president of the Cartoonists Guild and of the Northern California Cartoon and Humor Association. He and his wife, Mary Lou, live in Carmel, California, and are avid tennis players.

BO BROWN

Bo Brown is a native of Philadelphia and a Phi Beta Kappa graduate of the University of Pennsylvania. His work has appeared in more than 700 magazines and newspapers in the U.S. and abroad. He was named "Best Magazine Gag Cartoonist" of the year by the National Cartoonists Society in 1982. This caricature is how he thinks he looks.

FORD BUTTON

Ford Button recently retired from 31 years of teaching art in all levels of the New York State schools. He began cartooning as a hobby, but over a period of about 20 years it has become a full-time career. His work has appeared in such publications as *Saturday Review, Good Housekeeping, Wall Street Journal, Instructor*, and many trade, technical, and fraternal magazines. He is a World War II veteran and a sometime jazz musician.

MARTHA CAMPBELL

Martha Campbell is a graduate of Washington University School of Fine Arts and was formerly a writer/designer for Hallmark Cards. She has been a freelance cartoonist for 10 years, has illustrated three books, and has sold more than 2,000 cartoons. She is married to an attorney and has two children.

OTHA J. COLLINS

Otha J. Collins has been a teacher of art in the Portsmouth, Virginia, public schools for the past 20 years. For the last seven of those years he has been an aspiring freelance cartoonist and finds cartooning an excellent alternative to watching television at night. He lives in Portsmouth with his wife, Joann, and their two children.

FRANK COTHAM

Frank Cotham graduated from Memphis State University in 1971 with a Bachelor of Fine Arts degree that so far has impressed no one. He now works for WHBQ-TV, a local ABC affiliate in Memphis, Tennessee. Frank started drawing panel cartoons and sending them to magazines just for fun about four years ago and was shocked when *Saturday Review* actually bought one! Since then his work has appeared in such publications as *Saturday Evening Post, Punch,* and the *Wall Street Journal.* He lives with his wife and two children in Bartlett, Tennessee, a suburb of Memphis.

GLEN DINES

Glen Dines was born a number of years ago in Casper, Wyoming. He spent most of his time growing up in central Washington State. Today, he lives in Marin Country, California. Probably one of the few cartoonists who actually taught in public school — high school art and English — he has also written and/or illustrated some 20 juvenile titles and designed and written historical exhibits for national parks throughout the U.S. He is a real nice guy and a snappy dresser — as you can see from this photo.

JAMES ESTES

James Estes is 41 years old, married, and has three children — a boy and two girls. He has been cartooning full time for just over 13 years. His work has appeared in such national publications as the *Wall Street Journal, National Enquirer, Reader's Digest, Changing Times, Good Housekeeping, Boy's Life, Saturday Evening Post*, and the *Christian Science Monitor*. His own book of cartoons is called *Put a Smile in Your Eyes.*

DAVE GERARD

Dave Gerard has been a cartoonist since 1931. In 1966 he entered into a discussion with the Des Moines Register & Tribune Syndicate to introduce a panel feature for newspaper editorial pages that depicted the plight of the average citizen trying to battle inflation, taxes, city hall, mortgages, etc. "Citizen Smith" made its first appearance in April 1967 in nearly 100 newspapers. In 1971 Gerard was elected mayor of Crawfordsville, Indiana. He continued to draw "Citizen Smith." Since leaving the mayor's office on 1 January 1976, Gerard has gone back to the drawing board where he continues to draw "Citizen Smith" every day.

RANDY JAY GLASBERGEN

Randy Jay Glasbergen has been cartooning professionally since he was 15 years old. His work has appeared in *Good Housekeeping, New Woman, Cosmopolitan, Saturday Evening Post*, and many other magazines worldwide. Randy also writes and draws cartoons for nearly 200 daily and Sunday newspapers and does illustrations for greeting cards, books, magazines, and advertising agencies. He lives in rural upstate New York with his wife, two daughters, and enough pets to crowd an ark.

RANDY HALL

Randy Hall owns an antique and coin shop in Liberal, Kansas, and enjoys drawing cartoons in his spare time. His work has appeared in most major publications including *National Enquirer, New Woman, American Legion*, and *Cosmopolitan*. Randy and his wife Marlene enjoy antiquing, fishing, and golf.

SIDNEY HARRIS

Sidney Harris's cartoons have appeared in many national magazines and newspapers, including *ABA Press, American Scientist, Chicago Tribune, Playboy, Saturday Review, Wall Street Journal*, and *Science 80*. He has also published a number of cartoon collections, the most recent of which is *What's So Funny About Computers?* (William Kaufman, 1982).

NICK HOBART

Nick Hobart writes that he is too ugly to send a photo and too dull to send a biography. He does, however, send best wishes.

NORMAN HOIFJELD

Norman Hoifjeld is a graduate of Brooklyn College of CUNY and Teachers College of Columbia University. He taught for 25 years in the New York City school system, during which time he did considerable cartooning. His work has appeared in the *Saturday Evening Post, Ladies' Home Journal, Collier's, American, Good Housekeeping, Cosmopolitan, McCall's, Redbook, Argosy*, and many others.

JIM HULL

Jim Hull grew up in South Bend, Indiana, and graduated from Indiana Central University. He once hoped to be a silversmith but discovered that he enjoys cartooning more. It is his way of avoiding the seriousness of life. Drawing is second nature to him, and he finds the writing fascinating. He often tries to incorporate the literal meanings of words and phrases into his cartoons.

EDWIN LEPPER

Edwin Lepper was born in Springfield, Massachusetts, in 1913. He graduated from Amherst College in 1936, spent a short spell in the retail business, and served four years in the U.S. Army (1942-46). He did not begin cartooning until 1950 but hopes to continue till 198?. He does not have a recent photo and is hoping to get by with this 20-year-old one.

JAMES E. LINDENSMITH

James E. Lindensmith is 57 years old and lives in Big Bear Lake, Calif. He has been a full-time cartoonist for 25 years.

SELF PORTRAIT
WITH GLASSES
30 YEARS AGO

SELF PORTRAIT
WITHOUT GLASSES
TODAY

HENRY MARTIN

Henry Martin was born in Louisville, Kentucky, just 110 miles from Cincinnati, Ohio. Because he had not learned to fly, he fell from the nest at age 23 and landed on his head. That is, he became a cartoonist and moved to New Jersey. He and his wife, Edie, rented an apartment and began accumulating junk. Their two children, Ann and Jane, grew up surrounded by fond memories and garage sale items. When they could no longer stand it, they moved to New York.

TOM McCALLY

Tom McCally has been married for 28 of his 48 years. He has three children and two grandchildren. He has taught fifth through seventh grade for 20 years and has also taught night classes and a course in cartooning. He is a former student of the Famous Artists Schools correspondence course, and he holds a B.Ed. and an M.Ed. from the University of Toledo, Ohio.

JOEL PETT

Joel Pett has been editorial cartoonist and newsroom artist for the *Herald-Telephone* in Bloomington, Indiana, since 1978. His cartoons have appeared in numerous other publications, including the *Louisville Times* and *The Progressive*. A collection of his political cartoons, *Pett Peeves*, was published in 1982. He is a member of the Association of American Editorial Cartoonists and the Cartoonists Guild.

TONY SALTZMAN

Tony Saltzman was born in Muskegon, Michigan, in 1938 and has lived most of his life in Grand Rapids. He broke into the world of cartooning by accident. As a gag he put on an exhibit of insane drawings with shuffled titles from a book on French painting. Some nut bought the whole show. Tony started thinking. His work has since appeared in more than 300 magazines, including *TV Guide, Playboy, Modern Bride, Saturday Review*, and *Playbill*.

CLEM SCALZITTI

Clem Scalzitti, who is 50 years old, married, and has four children, has been a commercial artist since 1953. After an unsuccessful campaign for Congress in 1974, he took up cartooning full time to regain his sense of humor. His work has appeared in *New Woman, National Enquirer, Saturday Review, Changing Times, New York Times*, and most of the men's magazines.

JIM SCHMALZRIED

Jim Schmalzried is a cartoonist who lives quietly tucked away in rural Indiana.

PETER STEINER

Peter Steiner has been a cartoonist for six years. Before that, he was a professor of German at Dickinson College, Carlisle, Pa. His work has appeared in *The New Yorker, The Nation, Saturday Review*, and a number of other publications. He now does cartoons for the *Washington Times*.

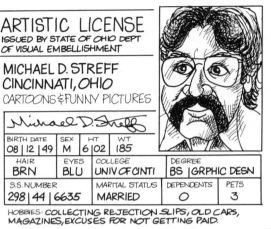

ARTISTIC LICENSE
ISSUED BY STATE OF OHIO DEPT
OF VISUAL EMBELLISHMENT

MICHAEL D. STREFF
CINCINNATI, OHIO
CARTOONS & FUNNY PICTURES

Michael D. Streff

BIRTH DATE	SEX	HT	WT
08	12	49	M	6	02	185

HAIR	EYES	COLLEGE	DEGREE
BRN	BLU	UNIV OF CINTI	BS	GRPHIC DESN

S.S. NUMBER	MARITAL STATUS	DEPENDENTS	PETS
298	44	6635	MARRIED	O	3

HOBBIES: COLLECTING REJECTION SLIPS, OLD CARS,
MAGAZINES, EXCUSES FOR NOT GETTING PAID.

BARDULF UELAND

Bardulf Ueland was born and raised in Halstad, Minnesota, and served in the U.S. Army in World War II and the U.S. Air Force Reserves in the Korean War. His cartoons have appeared in 90 publications. He holds degrees in art education from the University of North Dakota and Moorhead State University and has been an art instructor in the Fargo, North Dakota, public schools for 23 years. He is a member of the Moorhead, Minnesota/Fargo, North Dakota Chapter of Phi Delta Kappa.

CHUCK VADUN

Chuck Vadun is creative director of an advertising agency by day and a cartoonist by night. His work is syndicated nationally by United Features Syndicate to newspapers in the U.S. and foreign countries. His work has appeared in *Good Housekeeping, Saturday Evening Post, Wall Street Journal, Woman's World, National Enquirer*, and many others. When he is not drawing, he can be found on the basketball court pondering how a 5'8" cartoonist can learn to slam dunk. He is faithfully supported by his wife, Lynne; son, Chuck; and a cat and dog with ridiculous names.

JAN VAN WESSUM

Jan van Wessum was born in 1932 and has published cartoons in such U.S. and European publications as *Punch, Penthouse, Saturday Evening Post*, and the *New York Times*. In addition to cartooning, he also paints and etches.

W. A. VANSELOW

W. A. Vanselow, an active cartoonist for the past 40 years, got his start in cartooning under the personal guidance of W. L. Evans, the director of the world-famous correspondence cartoon course. After eight lessons Evans hired him to correct the lessons of his many students. He studied life drawing at John Huntington Polytechnic Institute in Cleveland, Ohio, under Rolfe Stoll. His work has been reproduced in many foreign publications and cartoon collections, including *Best Cartoons of the Year* for 10 years.

RAY VOGLER

Ray Vogler is a research artist for General Motors Research Laboratories. He freelances for fun, and his work has appeared in 200 publications. He has a dog, a cat, and 20 goldfish.